FISHING SKILLS

Fly Fishing for Trout

Tony Whieldon

Introduction by Russ Symons

WARD LOCK LIMITED · LONDON

© Ward Lock Limited 1984

First published in Great Britain in 1984
by Ward Lock Limited, 82 Gower Street,
London WC1E 6EQ, a Pentos Company.

Printed and bound in Italy by
New Interlitho, Milan

British Library Cataloguing in Publication Data

Whieldon, Tony
　　Flyfishing for trout.
　　1. Trout fishing—Pictorial works
　　2. Fly fishing—Pictorial works
　　I. Title　　II. Series
　　799.1′755　　SH687

　　ISBN 0-7063-6281-0

Contents

Acknowledgments
My thanks to Michael, Graham and Bob, whose invaluable
assistance made the marathon a little shorter.

Introduction

Fly fishing for trout is rightly regarded as the most subtle of the angling disciplines, and during the last two decades it has enjoyed a tremendous growth in popularity.

In the 1960s, a government decree mandated the water authorities to open their storage reservoirs to the public, thus greatly increasing the availability of good-quality trout fishing. From that moment, the boom in trout fishing gained momentum, and today it has become a highly valued recreational activity among many of this country's three million anglers. Indeed, increasing numbers of coarse and sea anglers gravitate to the reservoirs at the beginning of each season, to add fly fishing to their repertoire of fishing skills, and to have a change from their usual sport.

Whether you are a complete newcomer to fishing, or an experienced angler, it is essential, if you are to be a successful fly fisherman, that you are able to cast properly. In addition, a good casting style will enable you to fish with precision throughout a long day without becoming tired.

It is all too easy to fall into the trap of spending a lot of money on tackle before learning to cast. This can be a complete waste, and can set back your casting ability, and therefore your success rate, for years.

Your first rod can influence your style of casting for life. If a bad habit once becomes established, it will develop into a subconscious reflex. Before you know it, you will have a flaw in your technique

which may take yards off the distance at which you are able to present a fly. And all the time, you remain blissfully unaware that this is happening.

In order to cast properly, you must be using the rod that is best suited to you, and the best place to get advice on casting and tackle is at one of the many professional casting schools that now exist. No matter how well intentioned your friend is when he offers to teach you, go to a good casting school as early on as you can, and certainly before you splash out hard cash on tackle. See what the professional is using, ask his advice, try the different rods he will have available; this is all part of what you are paying for.

Carbon fibre rods have now become so cheap that when you do buy a rod, you would be well advised to go straight to this space-age material. The rod should preferably be over 9 ft (2.75 m) in length. It is more difficult to cast a short rod than a longer one, so don't buy a shorter rod in the mistaken belief that it will be easier to use. But in any event, and it bears repeating, go to a professional school and get some advice.

There is another important point about tackle that I should like to make, and it concerns fly lines. Hard-won, practical experience has proved that your choice of fly line makes all the difference between a blank day and a full bag.

A good-quality line matched to the casting power of your rod is vital to good casting. However, it is the way in which that line behaves in the water that will determine whether or not you catch your quota of fish. And before anyone gets the wrong idea, the most expensive line, in my opinion, is not always the best.

You should walk the bank of your local reservoir or river, observing what tackle the majority of fishermen are using. Is it a floating line or one that sinks? What colour line is most used? Have a natter with anglers who are resting. However, don't, whatever you do, interrupt someone who may be chasing a fish. Most anglers are polite, but in such circumstances you may suffer some verbal indignities (see the section on bankside etiquette). Ask the angler what number line he thinks is best, what make, what rod is he using, and so on. It is also a good idea to join the local angling club, as you can then ask other members for advice. When anglers have been sufficiently 'lubricated' you can learn a lot from them; in addition, you will probably be treated to many entertaining half-truths that have been stretched further than they have any right to be.

Another advantage to joining a club is that during the winter months it will probably run a fly-tying class. Your local adult education centre may also run one, and it is well worth the effort to attend. Not only will tying your own flies save you money, but also the experience of landing a good fish on a fly which you have tied yourself is one of the most satisfying aspects of fly fishing. At first you will be tempted to try your hand at all sorts of wonderfully fluffy, highly-coloured lures, but over the years it is the simple, easily-tied flies which have endured and caught fish for generations of fly fishermen.

Make sure, when you step forth onto the bank for the first time, that your fly wallet is well stocked with classically simple flies, such as the legendary Black and Peacock spider, stick fly, worm fly, sedge pupa, and a few simply-tied lures, such as the Sweeny Todd, Black lure and Appetiser. These will be sufficient to catch fish under most conditions. Indeed a few of the very best fly fishermen rarely use more than half a dozen patterns right through the season, and catch just as many fish as any of us: a classic example of the rule which applies to all forms of fishing, 'Keep it simple and straightforward'.

When the author, Tony Whieldon, asked me to write this introduction to his book, I was both honoured and a little horrified at the task, because I know him to be a very able fly fisherman. What he has done in this book, as well as to demonstrate his superb draughtsmanship, is to show you his down-to-earth grasp of the information you need to know to catch trout, and I know he will join with me in wishing you 'Tight Lines'.

Russ Symons,
Plymouth, Devon.

January 1984.

Rods

Modern fly rods are man-
ufactured in glass fibre,
carbon fibre and boron.
Carbon rods are always
recognizable by their slim
butt area just in front of the
handle. The slimness belies
their power for they are quite
capable of throwing a line
40 yds (35 m) or more.

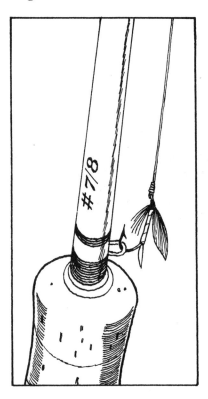

Just above the handle, on
the rod itself, a number will
show the manufacturer's recommended line size for use
with the rod.

In this instance a size 7 or
8 line would be suitable.

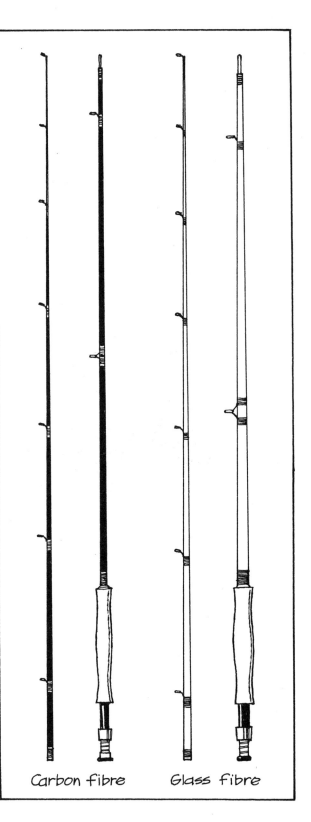

Carbon fibre   Glass fibre

Reels

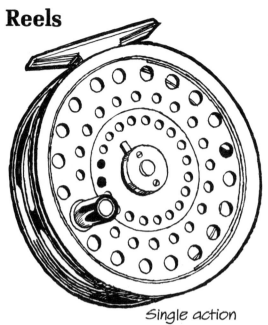

Single action

As the original function of the fly reel is to store line in a convenient package, this reel with its uncluttered design is the one used and favoured by the majority of fly fishermen.

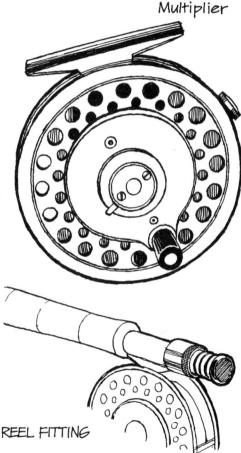

Multiplier

MULTIPLIER
For extra-fast line retrieve this reel excels. If you prefer this design, as many do, frequent lubrication will prolong its efficiency.

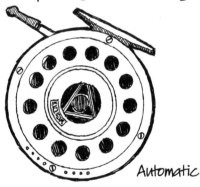

Automatic

AUTOMATIC
This reel strips line back on to the spool very fast, with the aid of a spring mechanism. Simply press the lever to keep in touch with a fast moving fish which is heading towards you.

REEL FITTING

It is a matter of choice which way the reel is secured. Some anglers have the handle on the right side, while others prefer a left-handed wind.

Lines

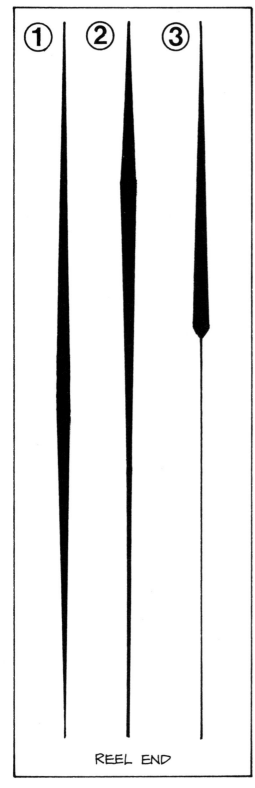

REEL END

① DOUBLE TAPER
   The standard length for a fly line is 30yd (27·43m). For delicate presentation for close to medium-distance casting the DT is ideal. The economical advantage of this line is that it can be reversed, as each end is a mirror image of the other.

② WEIGHT FORWARD
   Longer casts can be produced with this line, but with the drawback that when the line alights on the water surface quite a disturbance is created.

③ SHOOTING HEAD
   This consists of what is virtually a double-taper line cut in half with an ample supply of much finer backing or shooting line tied to the rear end. It is capable of producing very long-distance casts.

Lines

FLOATING

This line sits on the surface of the water. It is used when fish are feeding on or near the surface. It can also be used in conjunction with a weighted nymph to seek out fish that are feeding close to the bottom.

SINK TIP

A floating line with about 10ft (3·05m) of sinking line at the forward end. Ideal for nymph fishing.

SLOW SINKING

This is a very useful line for searching different depths or for fishing a lure or a nymph at mid-water.

FAST SINKING

If the trout are feeding on or near the bottom in deep water, this is the line to use.

VERY FAST SINK, AND LEAD CORE

This line sinks very quickly and is invaluable for use in very deep water when the fishing is being done from a boat. Lead core is the ideal line for trolling a big lure behind a rowed boat.

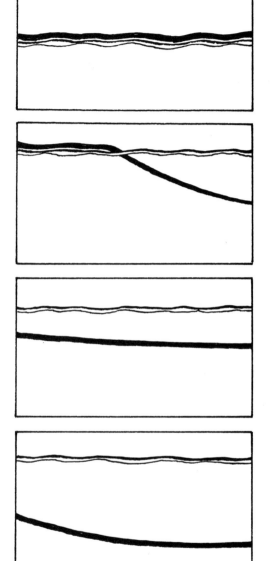

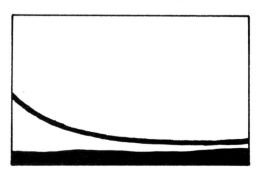

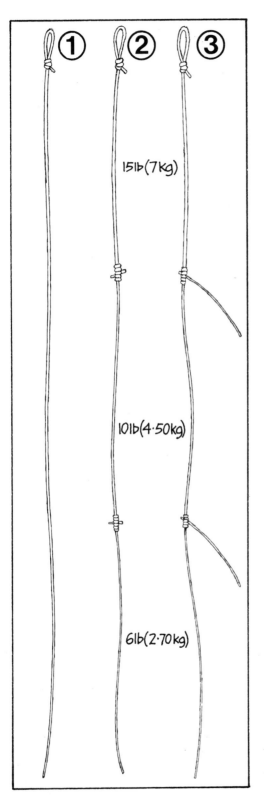

Leaders

① KNOTLESS TAPER
   For fine fly presentation these are the best, but they have one drawback; during the course of use, and after a number of flies have been changed, they obviously become shorter. This means that what started as a leader with, say, a 4lb (1·80kg) point will eventually become a leader with a 5lb (2·25kg) or a 6lb (2·70kg) point.

② KNOTTED TAPER
   Many anglers today purchase small spools of nylon of different breaking strains and make their own. All that is then required to maintain the length is a new section of nylon at the point, which is connected to the rest of the leader via a blood knot.

③ TAPERED WITH TWO DROPPERS
   This type of leader is mainly used for fishing loch-style from a drifting boat, although there is no reason why it should not be used from the bank.

   The breaking strains shown are typical of what may be used when fishing a water where the trout run to around 10lb (4·50 kg) in weight. A finer section of, say, 4lb (1·80kg) may be added if the trout are smaller, or when using very small flies.

Connecting line to leader

It is convenient to have a permanent coupling length of nylon about 24in (60cm) long fastened to the end of the fly line. When a new leader is required it is a quick and easy operation to replace it. The standard overall length of the leader should be about the same length as the rod. If fishing a leaded nymph from a floating line over deep water, the leader would obviously have to be longer.

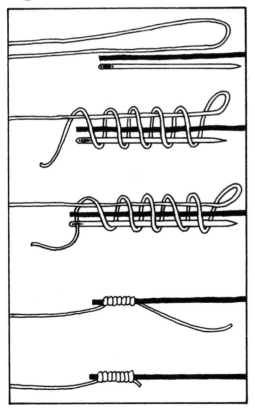

Knot for fastening leader to line and line to backing.

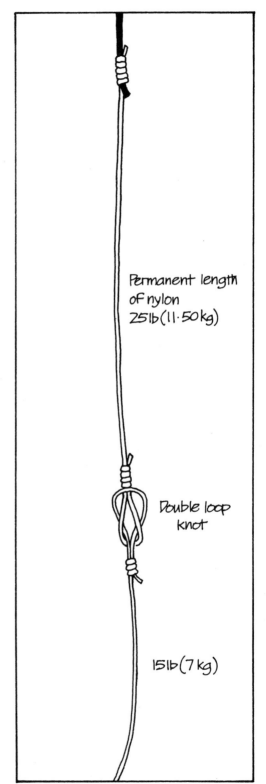

Permanent length of nylon 25lb (11.50kg)

Double loop knot

15lb (7kg)

Backing

As the overall length of a fly line is no more than 30yd (27m), it is necessary to increase the volume of line on the reel by adding several yards of backing. The amount of backing required will depend on the size of the reel. Wide-drum reels are generally used for lake fishing and obviously take more line than a standard spool, which is normally used for fishing on small to medium rivers. To find the answer, wind the fly line on to the spool, attach the backing to the line, then wind the backing on to the reel until it lies about ⅛in (3mm) beneath the housing supports. Remove the backing and line from the reel, reverse, and wind on again, backing first. Attach the backing to the spool with the knot shown below.

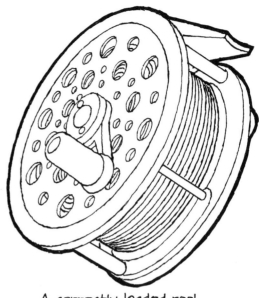

A correctly loaded reel

It is customary, when fishing still-waters, to have a selection of reels, each loaded with a different line. This will allow the angler to cope with the varied conditions and fish behaviour encountered on lakes.

When fishing on running water, a floating line is usually sufficient.

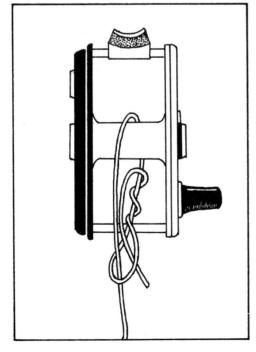

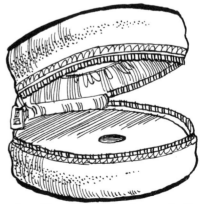

Look after your reels and they won't let you down. Reel cases keep out grit and dust which could harm the mechanism of the reel and the coating of the line.

Fly hooks

SPROAT hooks with a turned-down eye are probably the most ideally suited hook for the traditional wet fly patterns.

SPROAT hooks with a turned-up eye are used for dry flies, although some anglers prefer dry flies tied on the down-eyed hook.

Lures, and most nymphs are tied on long shanked hooks with a turned-down eye.

6   8   10   12   14   16   18

4   6   8   10   12

Artificial flies

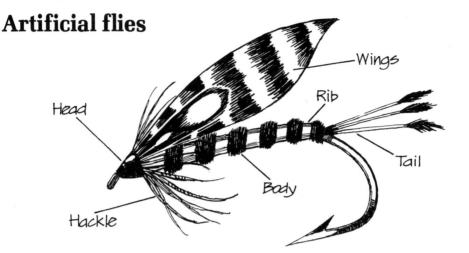

Wings

Rib

Head

Tail

Body

Hackle

DRY FLIES

Used when fish are taking insects from the surface. Equally effective on river and lake. Most dry flies are tied with the purpose of imit-ating, as closely as possible, a part-icular species of insect.

WET FLIES

Some of the traditional wet fly patterns bear some resemblance to aquatic life, but on the whole they are bright and flashy. The smaller, hackled wet flies used by the river angler for upstream fishing are, on the other hand, most life-like.

LURES

These probably account for more stillwater trout than all the other types combined, mainly because of their more widespread use. Colours used in their construction are as varied as the spectrum. They rep-resent small fish rather than aqua-tic insect life.

NYMPHS

Mostly fished in conjunction with a floating line. Some patterns are weighted by the inclusion of lead wire beneath the body material. Of all the artificials, these are the most life-like. Patterns vary from the very small buzzer pupae up to the large damselfly nymphs.

Mayflies

These artificials represent the largest of the British mayflies, *Ephemera danica*, which appears on rivers and lakes during May, June or July.

Fan-winged Mayfly

Partridge

Hackled Spinner

Hackle-point Spent Spinner

Popper lure

Anything less like a fly is hard to imagine, but this cork headed creation can be cast well enough with orthodox fly gear, and accounts for many good trout.

Use in conjunction with a floating line and retrieve with long steady pulls, across the water surface.

Dry flies

Black Gnat

Hawthorn

Hares Ear

Grey Duster

Knotted Midge

Alder

Coch-y-Bonddu

Baigent's Black

Walker's Sedge

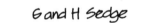

G and H Sedge

Greenwell's Glory

Pheasant Tail

Daddy Longlegs

Coachman

Iron Blue Dun

Blue Upright

Dark Varient

Wickham's Fancy

Red Spinner

Silver Sedge

Wet flies

Butcher

Dunkeld

Black Zulu

Black and Peacock

Peter Ross

Invicta

Mallard and Claret

Grenadier

Silver March Brown

Black Spider

Teal and Red

Wickham's Fancy

Blae and Black

Teal and Green

Teal Blue and Silver

Alexandra

Coachman

Red Palmer

Parson Hughes

Black Pennell

Lures

Ace of Spades

Appetizer

Missionary

Jack Frost

Muddler Minnow

Church Fry

Baby Doll

Polystickle

Sweeny Todd

Whisky Fly

Lures

Worm Fly

Black and Orange Marabou

Badger Lure

Black Lure

Dog Nobbler

Jersey Herd

Perch Fry

Undertaker

Matuka

Elver Lure

Nymphs

Amber Nymphs

Mayfly Nymph

Damselfly Nymph

Pheasant Tail Nymph

Damsel Wiggle Nymph

Stick Fly

Collyer's Nymph

Montana Stone

Persuader

Brown Caddis

Nymphs and pupae

Midge Pupae

Footballer

Leaded Shrimp

Chompers

Corixa

Corixa (Plastazote)

Longhorns

Iven's Nymph

PVC Nymph

Sedge Pupae

Sawyer's Pheasant Tail Nymph

Bloodworm

Silver Nymph

Alder Larva

Cove's Pheasant Tail

Casting a fly

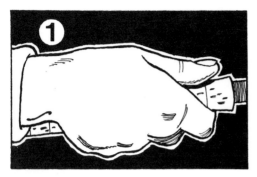

①

Hold the rod with the thumb on top of the handle....

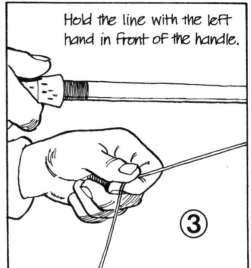

Hold the line with the left hand in front of the handle.

③

.... then pull enough line from the reel to provide enough weight to get the rod working properly.

②

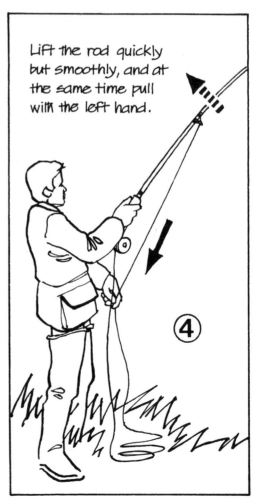

Lift the rod quickly but smoothly, and at the same time pull with the left hand.

④

Casting a fly

⑤ Stop the rod here. A common fault with many beginners is to let the rod fall back well beyond this point.

Pause in this position and let the line straighten out to the rear. If it helps, watch the line in the air.

⑥

⑦ Drive the rod forward....

.... and as the line unfurls over the water, release the line from the left hand, the 'shoot'!

⑧

Fishing a floating line

When the fish are active up in the surface area, and especially if you can see insects being blown on to the water surface, and being taken by the fish, it is worth using a dry fly.

Before the fly is cast, it should be 'dunked' in a bottle of floatant.

Dragging the fly across the surface in short erratic jerks will often produce a response.

A floating line can also be used to fish a nymph on or very near the bottom. In this case the leader will have to be longer than usual, (15ft (4.55m), and the nymph will need a weighted body (leaded nymph).

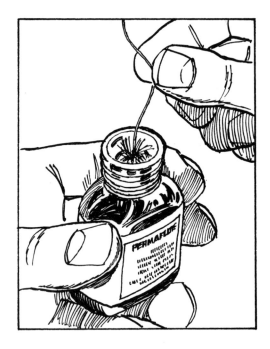

Whenever nymphs are being used, it is advisable to give the leader a wipe with 'leader sink'; a good substitute is washing-up liquid.

Fishing a floating line

Sometimes a trout will be seen leaving a trail of rings as it cruises just beneath the surface, sucking down insects which lie in its path. By logical deduction, it is possible to place your offering accurately ahead of the fish.

Next estimated rise

Present fly here

As nymphs or pupae rise to the surface to hatch, they are often intercepted by the fish before they reach the surface. This activity is perceptible only to the keenest eye. Binoculars are a great help when trout are feeding like this.

After the cast, pause awhile to let your nymph sink well beneath the surface, then retrieve line very slowly, pausing occasionally to keep the nymph about 12 in (30 cm) under the surface film.

Fishing a sinking line

Of the different types of sinking line the very slow sinker is the most versatile. It can be used to overcome a cross-wind problem, or to fish a nymph or lure in the upper layers of water, or over weedbeds and underwater snags.

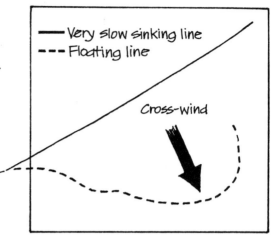

— Very slow sinking line
--- Floating line

Cross-wind

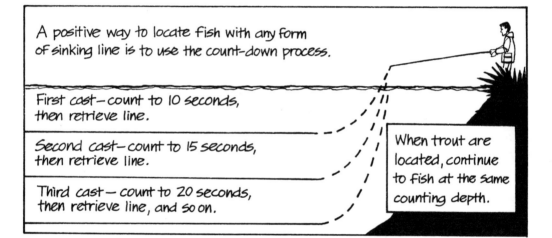

A positive way to locate fish with any form of sinking line is to use the count-down process.

First cast—count to 10 seconds, then retrieve line.

Second cast—count to 15 seconds, then retrieve line.

Third cast—count to 20 seconds, then retrieve line, and so on.

When trout are located, continue to fish at the same counting depth.

The way to retrieve a lure

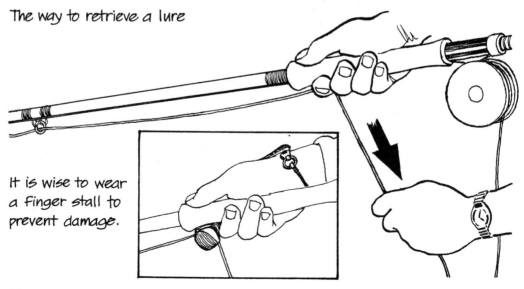

It is wise to wear a finger stall to prevent damage.

Although the very slow-sinking line is versatile it would not be practical to use it exclusively, as it would take far too long to sink to fish that were lying well down in very deep water.

When searching for fish in these deeper places use a fast, or very fast sinking line.

Fishing a sinking line

When retrieving a lure, especially quickly, it is important to hold the rod correctly in relation to the line. Some trout will take a lure in a very savage manner. It is therefore best to hold the rod at an angle to the line, in order to cushion the shock of a taking trout.

WRONG

CORRECT

Species

BROWN TROUT (Salmo trutta fario)
   This trout is indigenous to Great Britain and Europe, and is found wherever the water has a high oxygen content, from the acid streams of high ground to the more alkaline waters of lower ground. Acid-water trout seldom grow to any great size, unless they have an unusually rich food supply.

RAINBOW TROUT (Salmo gairdneri)
   Introduced to Europe and Britain in the 1880s, it is used extensively to stock man-made fisheries, but does not breed, except in a few places where the conditions are exactly suitable. Distinguishable by the magenta stripe along the flank.

AMERICAN BROOK TROUT (Salvelinus fontinalis)
   This fish is more a char than a trout but can be cross-bred with both the brown and the rainbow trout. A brook/brown trout cross is known as a 'tiger trout.'

Cannibal trout

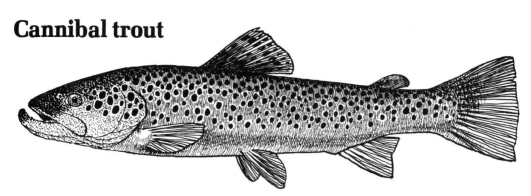

Old male trout very seldom bother to feed on surface-borne insect life, except, perhaps, when a heavy hatch of *Ephemera danica* is taking place.

They adopt, instead, a diet consisting of small coarse fish and trout. The nomenclator is very apt, for they can be as rapacious as any pike.

Ghost Swift

These predatory trout can be caught on lures. The perch-fry streamer is probably the best bet. At dusk and during the night they often swim near the surface, and can be caught on an imitation ghost-swift moth.

Anatomy of a trout

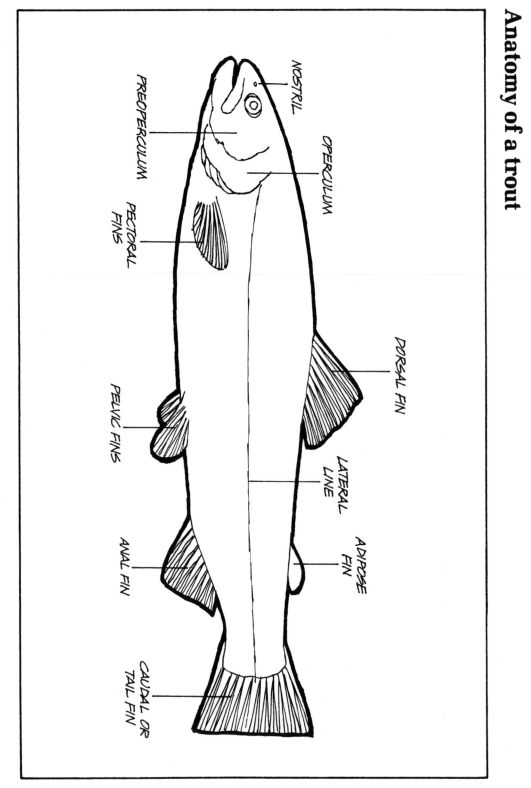

NOSTRIL

PREOPERCULUM

OPERCULUM

PECTORAL FINS

DORSAL FIN

PELVIC FINS

LATERAL LINE

ADIPOSE FIN

ANAL FIN

CAUDAL OR TAIL FIN

EPHEMEROPTERA (Mayflies)

The trout's diet

Members of this group of insects all have upright wings and two or three long tails. There are four stages in the metamorphosis: egg, nymph, sub-imago and imago. Fishermen refer to the sub-imago as the 'dun', and to the imago as the 'spinner'.

At the surface the 'dun' emerges from the nymphal skin.

The 'spinner' then emerges from the 'dun'.

After mating, the eggs are deposited into the water, and both male and female fall to the water surface as 'spent spinners'.

Nymphs are also taken by trout as they swim towards the surface.

These dead and dying flies are easy prey for trout.

After hatching from the egg the nymph lives and feeds on the bottom. Some are eaten at this stage by foraging trout.

Other groups of insects go through a similar sort of development as the Ephemeroptera. All the stages shown below form part of the trout's diet.

The trout's diet

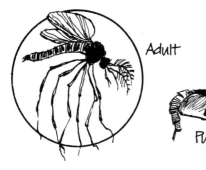
Adult

DIPTERA: In this group, the midges (Chironomids) are of most interest to trout.

Pupa   Larva   Larva (bloodworm)

TRICHOPTERA: This group includes the caddis or sedge flies.

Caddis larvae in cases

Pupa

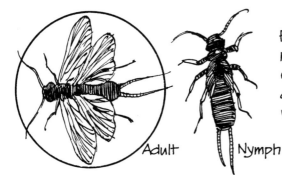
Adult

PLECOPTERA: These are found mainly in stony rivers. The nymph of the large adult stonefly is very active, and is a main food item where it occurs.

Adult   Nymph

ZYGOPTERA: Adult damselflies are occasionally taken by trout, but the nymph is a main food item.

Nymph

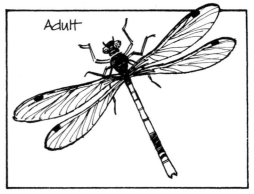
Adult

The trout's diet

Many other species of non-aquatic insects form part of the trout's diet. These are blown on to the surface of the water by the wind. Here are the two most commonly encountered.

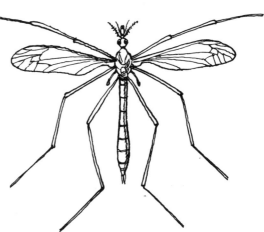

Crane-fly or 'daddy-long-legs'.

Hawthorn fly (artificial).

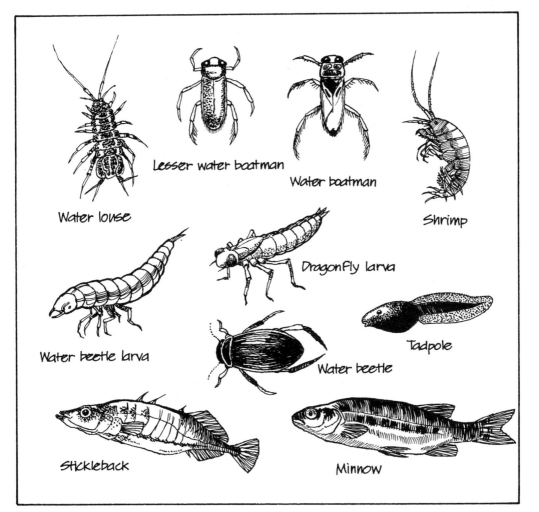

Water louse

Lesser water boatman

Water boatman

Shrimp

Water beetle larva

Dragonfly larva

Water beetle

Tadpole

Stickleback

Minnow

Fishing a midge pupa

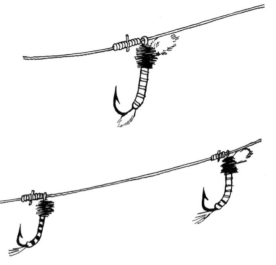

This artificial is meant to represent the pupae of chironomidae (midges) which hang in the surface film before their final metamorphosis into the adult midge (buzzer).

To ensure that the artificial hangs stationary in the surface film, the leader should be greased so that it floats. Mount two or three on the leader, each one stopped by a blood knot. Tie a sedge, well treated with floatant, on the point to act as an additional buoy.

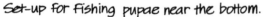

Set-up for fishing pupae near the bottom.

Midge pupae can also be fished in the traditional style, and retrieved very slowly.

Strike when the sedge disappears.

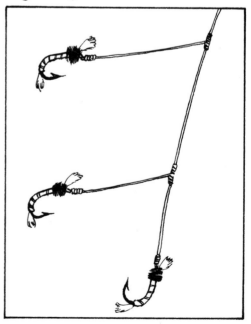

Fishing a sedge pupa

This pattern is a general representation of the many different sedge pupae found in most still-waters. During the summer months, the natural swims to the surface, or to the shore, in order to undergo the final transformation and become an adult sedge fly.

The artificial can be fished at midwater, or near the bottom with a sinking line ....

.... or just under the surface with a floating, sink-tip, or very slow-sinking line.

Retrieve the pupa at a medium pace, with long steady pulls, and a pause here and there.

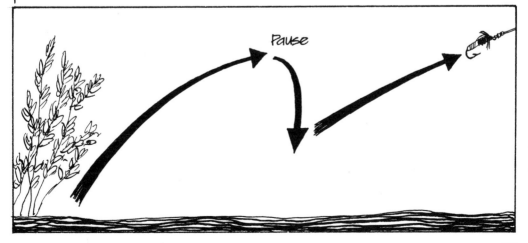

Pause

Fishing a damselfly nymph

During the early part of the season this pattern can be fished, very slowly, along the bottom. Shallower bays, where weed is prolific during the summer, are the most likely areas to attract the natural nymphs, as they feed largely on decaying vegetable matter.

During the warmer months the nymphs are far more active and wriggle to the surface, whereupon they proceed to swim towards the shore or surface weed in order to hatch into adult damselflies. To sim- ulate this activity, fish the artificial just under the surface with a fairly fast retrieve, on a floating line.

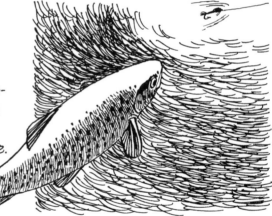

Where there are rushes or reeds, it is often more productive to cast and retrieve along the shoreline.

Fishing a daddy-long-legs

The crane fly or 'daddy-long-legs' is a familiar sight at the water-side from June onwards. They are often blown onto the water surface where they struggle in their attempts to become air-borne once more. Such a large insect presents a good mouthful to the trout, which respond avidly.

Cast the artificial to an area where trout activity is obvious on the surface, (the fly will need to be well 'dunked' in floatant), then just wait for a fish to find it.

When a take does occur, resist the temptation to strike, as the trout will often try to drown the fly first, before taking it in its mouth.

Wait until the line starts to run out, then lift the rod high to set the hook.

Drag a 'daddy-long-legs' through a heavy ripple, or waves, and the trout will often respond with a very positive take.

Fishing a corixa

This pattern imitates the lesser water-boatman which spends most of its life near the bed of the lake, but has to rise to the surface in order to replenish its air supply.

Two patterns have developed to represent this little bug. The leaded version, which can be fished via a floating or a sinking line close to the bottom...

... and the buoyant (plastazote) version, which has to be fished with a sinking line.

Cast the buoyant corixa and allow the line to sink — the corixa will float on or near the surface.

When the line is retrieved, the corixa will dive towards the bottom, imitating, in a very life-like manner, the action of a water-boatman as it swims back to base.

Fishing a leaded shrimp

This pattern represents the fresh-water shrimp, Gammarus; a resident of well-oxygenated water. They thrive in watercress, suggesting therefore that lakes fed by streams containing this plant would be ideal places to use this very effective little pattern.

The combination of lead wire and the shape of the body results in the artificial adopting an inverted attitude, which simulates the natural in a very life-like manner.

A leaded shrimp is ideally suited for margin fishing in clear-water lakes. Let the shrimp sink to the bottom where trout are patrolling.

When a trout approaches, inch the shrimp off the bottom in short jerks.

Lake fishing

Protective clothing is of vital importance to the angler who fishes the exposed banks of large still-water fisheries.

A waxed proofed cotton jacket complete with hood and storm collar will keep the elements at bay. Thigh waders will keep the legs warm and dry. Make sure that the jacket hangs well down over the top of the waders.

The tackle bag should be large and roomy to accommodate, apart from spare reels etc., the large fly box which is necessary to hold the comprehensive selection of flies and lures that is required for lake fishing.

Lake fishing from the bank

The expanse of an unfamiliar lake may pose a problem to a visiting angler, but if he applies his knowledge and experience of other lakes to this one, he will soon locate fish. For every lake, whether it is man-made or natural, has features in common with other lakes, as well as its own personal characteristics. Here are some places well worth attention.

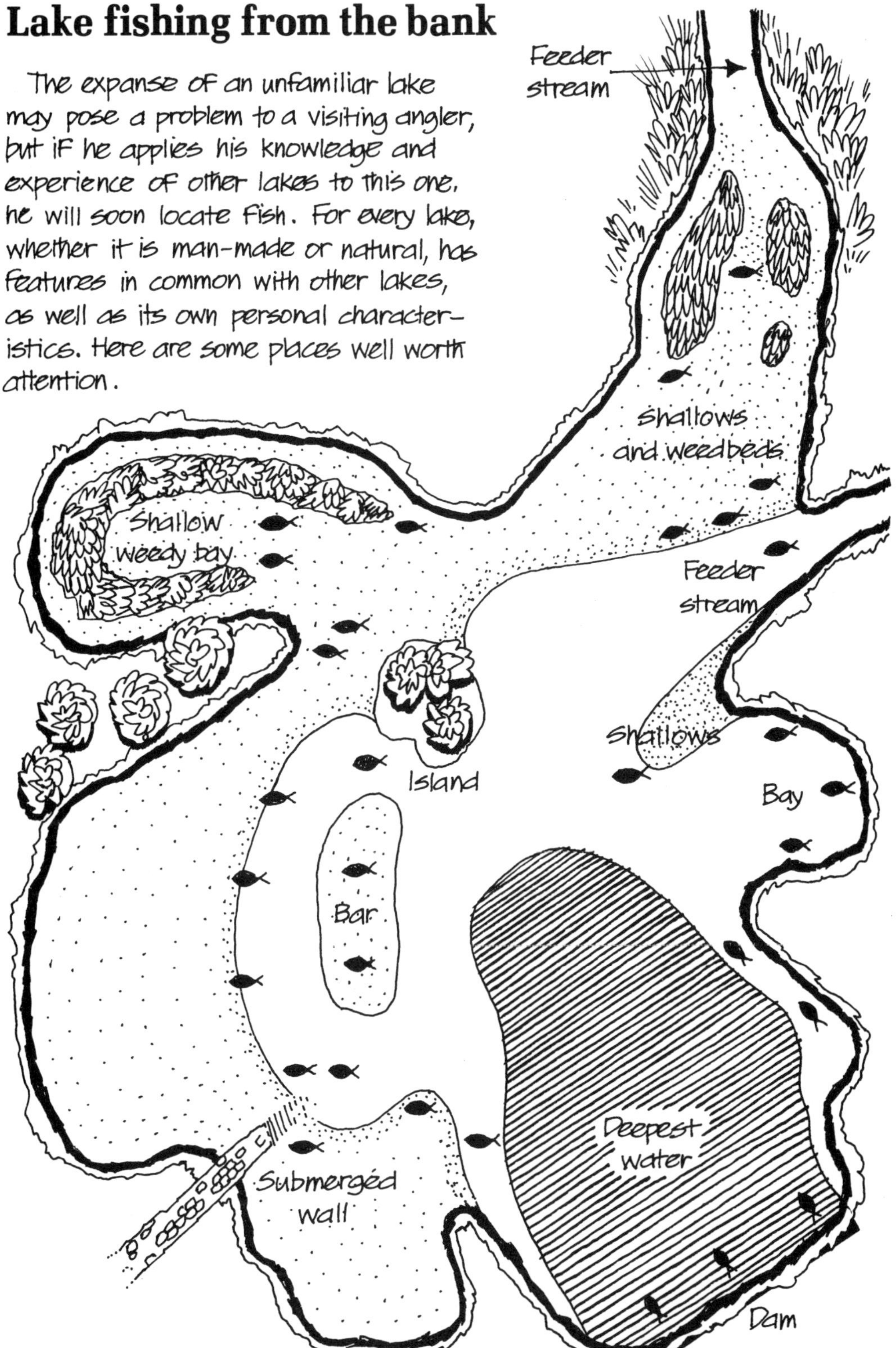

Feeder stream

Shallows and weedbeds

Shallow weedy bay

Feeder stream

Shallows

Island

Bay

Bar

Deepest water

Submerged wall

Dam

Using the wind

The wind can often be of assistance in the location of fish. Warm winds from the south, and south-west are best, both for fish and fishermen.

A left handed caster would be more comfortable here.

Dam and deep water

With a strong wind in this direction, the best fishing spot would be about here, with the wind over the left shoulder.

Wind direction

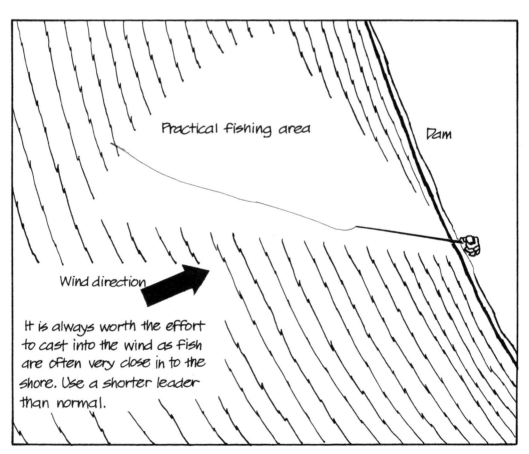

Practical fishing area

Dam

Wind direction

It is always worth the effort to cast into the wind as fish are often very close in to the shore. Use a shorter leader than normal.

Lake fishing from the bank

When fish are showing on the surface, they are usually feeding on
insects which have been blown on to
the water surface from the shore,
or on nymphs or pupae hanging in
the surface film.

If there are a number of fish
rising fairly close together, cast
among them and work the fly back
slowly in very short jerks.

Method of retrieving a small fly or
or nymph with a floating line.

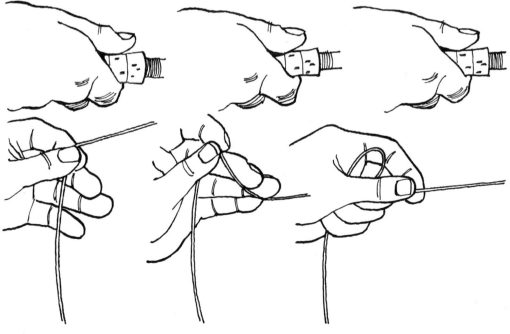

Fishing a lure from the bank

Hungry, early-season trout will grab almost any lure that is cast into a lake. Some lakes at this time of year tend to carry a certain amount of colour, which demands the use of a high-visibility lure, such as a Jack Frost, Appetizer, Ace of Spades or Dog Nobbler.

As the season advances, however, the food supply is more abundant, and the trout become more selective. Nymphs and flies are then the main items of food, but where fish fry exist these are also taken, and it is possible to imitate them with a lure. The shallows of many lakes support a healthy population of sticklebacks, minnows and other small fry on which the trout feed.

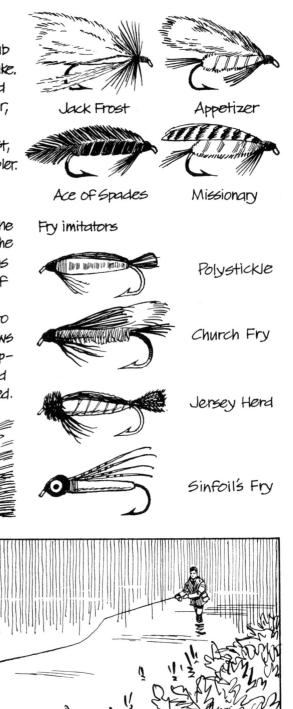

High visibility lures

Jack Frost

Appetizer

Ace of Spades

Missionary

Fry imitators

Polystickle

Church Fry

Jersey Herd

Sinfoil's Fry

Where fry activity is seen, cast a fry lure along the shore-line.

Fishing a lure from the bank

The Dog Nobbler is rather unusual inasmuch as it carries a whole split-shot as part of its dressing. It certainly does not represent anything in particular, but when drawn through the water it has a very stimulating action.

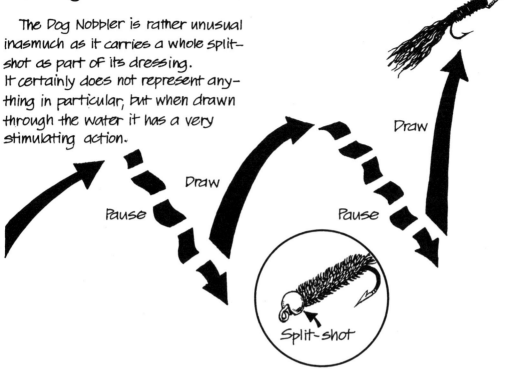

Draw

Draw

Pause

Pause

Split-shot

Another unique lure is the Muddler Minnow, which has the tendency to float, rather than sink like the Dog Nobbler. In medium-depth water it works better on a floating line; but in deep water, a slow-sinking line is more suitable if the fish are swimming deeper.

Lake fishing from a boat

The traditional loch style of fishing from a drifting boat is still very widely practised, and accounts for many good fish.

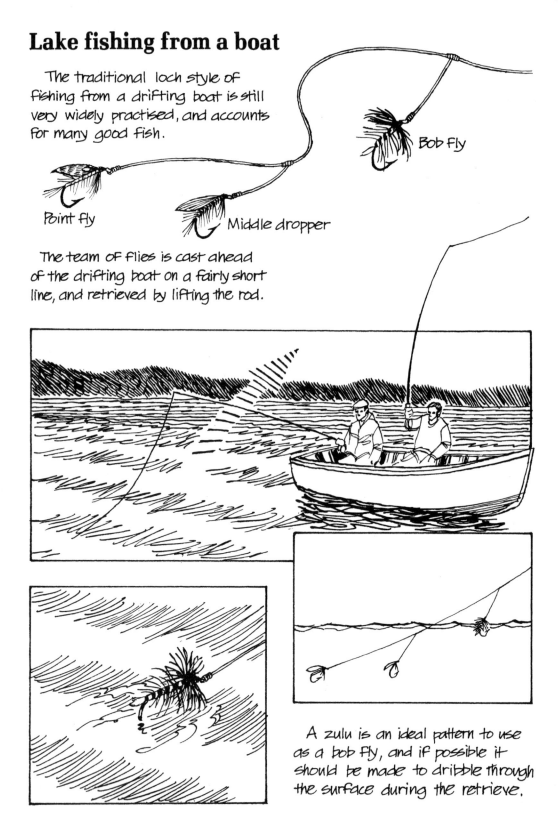

Bob Fly

Point fly

Middle dropper

The team of flies is cast ahead of the drifting boat on a fairly short line, and retrieved by lifting the rod.

A zulu is an ideal pattern to use as a bob fly, and if possible it should be made to dribble through the surface during the retrieve.

Wind and drift

The drift is usually performed along, and not too far out from, the shore-line. When the boat is drifting too quickly a drogue can be used to check its progress.

Drift →

Suggested patterns and positions

POINT	MIDDLE DROPPER	BOB
Butcher	Invicta	Zulu
Dunkeld	Mallard and Claret	Invicta
Peter Ross	Silver March Brown	Red Palmer
Teal Blue and Silver	Teal and Red	Greenwells Glory
Alexandra	Wickhams Fancy	Black and Peacock Spider

Lake fishing from a boat

Casting a dry fly to rising trout is a delightful form of boat-fishing.

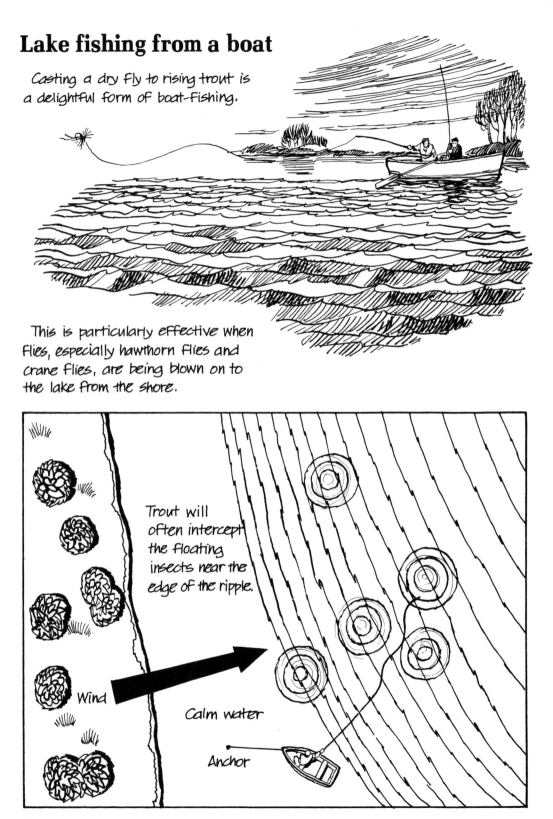

This is particularly effective when flies, especially hawthorn flies and crane flies, are being blown on to the lake from the shore.

Trout will often intercept the floating insects near the edge of the ripple.

Wind

Calm water

Anchor

Dapping with a daddy-long-legs

Dapping with a natural daddy-long-legs has been a method of angling practised for many years, on some Irish and Scottish lochs.

Given the right conditions, this form of fishing can be applied to most stillwater fisheries. There is no need to use the natural insect either—an artificial 'daddy' works just as well.

The boat is allowed to drift before the wind, just as with the loch-style of wet fly fishing. The rod, however, needs to be as long as possible in order to present plenty of line to the wind.

20 yds (18·30 m) of 'blow line'

6 ft (1·85 m) leader

Simply let the line blow out over the water, and attempt to keep the fly dancing in the waves.

With this method, an over-hasty strike will result in a missed fish. Wait until the trout has turned down with the fly in its mouth, then just tighten up.

Lure fishing from a boat is un-doubtably a very productive form of trout fishing. A single lure can be fished just beneath the surface, at mid-water, or on the bottom.

Lure fishing from a boat

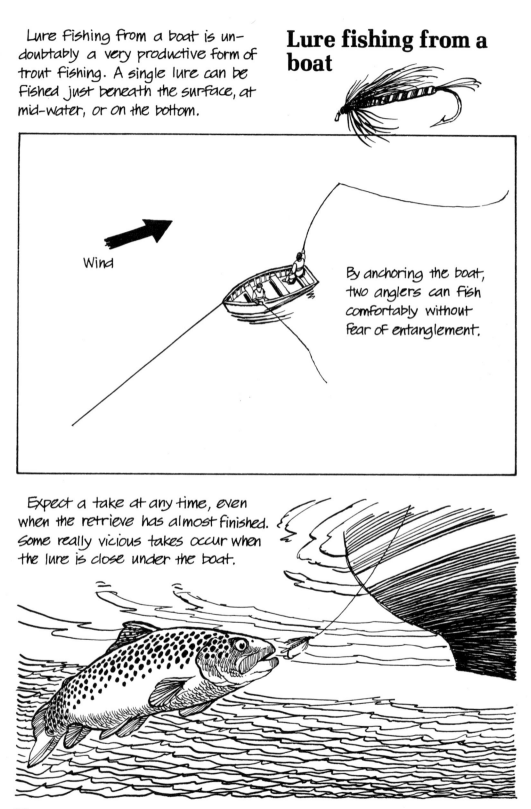

Wind

By anchoring the boat, two anglers can fish comfortably without fear of entanglement.

Expect a take at any time, even when the retrieve has almost finished. Some really vicious takes occur when the lure is close under the boat.

Trolling

This method involves trailing a lure about 30–40 yd (28-36 m) behind a rowing boat. A lead core line is used to keep the lure well down in the water. Lures used for this sort of fishing are usually of the tandem variety.

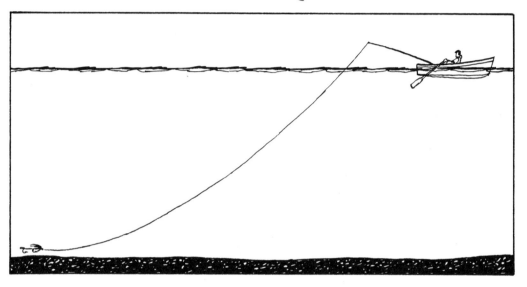

Trout caught with this method are generally larger than average.

River and stream fishing

Trout can be found in most rivers and streams where the water is clean. The trout of the fast rocky streams of the higher ground are usually small in comparison to the fish of the lowland rivers. Because of the turbulent nature of the rocky stream, wet fly fishing is the method most widely employed. On the lowland river, where the flow is more sedate, the dry fly is favoured.

— Moorland stream

Lowland stream

River and stream fishing

There is no need for a heavy line when fishing a stream. No's. 4, 5 or 6 will be ideal. A light coloured line will show up far better in the shadows of overhanging foliage.

Other items needed will include; waders, strong tackle bag with a wide shoulder strap, collapsible landing net, priest, fly floatant, leader sink (if nymph fishing), scissors, spare leaders and a selection of flies.

River and stream fishing

The successful river fly-fisherman is the one who moves with stealth, and remains outside the trout's field of vision.

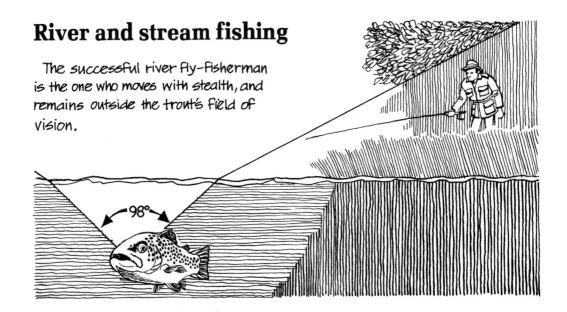

In very clear water, a trout lying near the river bed will have a larger field of vision than a trout lying near the surface.

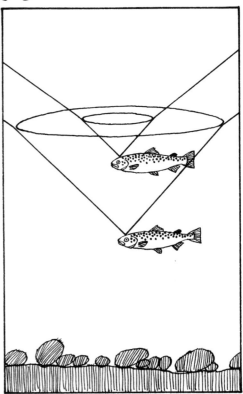

It is obvious from the above diagram that the only blind spot is directly to the rear of the trout. Whenever possible, approach the fish from that direction; especially when fishing in a confined area such as is commonly encountered on small overgrown streams.

Drab clothing merges with the background, and aids concealment, even when the angler is in the trout's field of vision.

Olive-green, waxed cotton jackets, or army surplus combat jackets are ideal.

It is often necessary to wade, even on small streams. Again, olive-green is the best colour to choose for waders, and they should not have studs. A better grip may be provided by studs on some surfaces, but they produce such a clatter on stones and pebbles that the trout can detect the vibration yards away.

Waders with cleated rubber soles are best for stalking trout.

Concealment

The ideal position to be in, when wading a pool, is tucked away under the bank. For safety's sake, always tread very carefully; even small streams contain deep and sudden drop-offs into nasty holes. There is nothing as effective as a wader full of water for dampening the spirits.

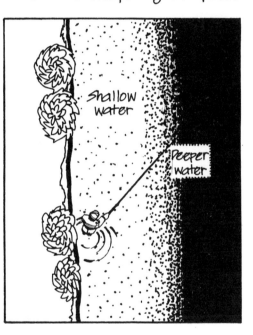

Shallow water

Deeper water

FIRM SILT OR SAND

The ideal material for wading on; muffles sound very efficiently.

ROCK

Cleated soles are silent on this, but it can be slippery.

PEBBLES

The worst base for stalking on. It is very noisy and sends shock waves right through a pool.

Fly presentation

When fishing in the confines of an overgrown stream the overhead cast is seldom practical. Instead, use the side cast.

The principal and timing of the side cast are the same as those of the overhead cast.

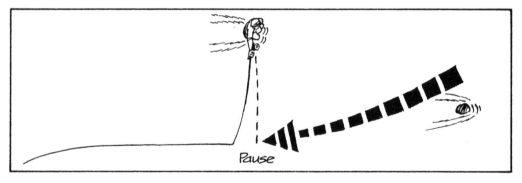

Pause

Work the line on an imaginary plane between overhanging foliage and the water surface.

When fishing a dry fly, wet fly or nymph directly upstream, or across and up, the angler has to recover line at the speed of the current in order to maintain contact with the fly.

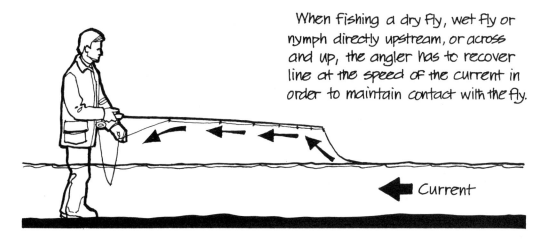

Current

When fishing from the bank on a small stream, with a short line on the water, the same effect can be achieved by moving the rod.

Current ➡

Fly lands here.

Lift off for next cast here.

Presentation of a floating fly directly downstream.

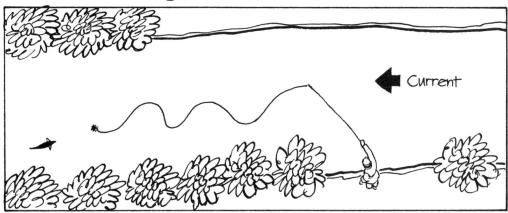

Current

Trout in a river always lie with their heads facing upstream, so it therefore makes sense to approach them from the rear, gradually working your way upstream.

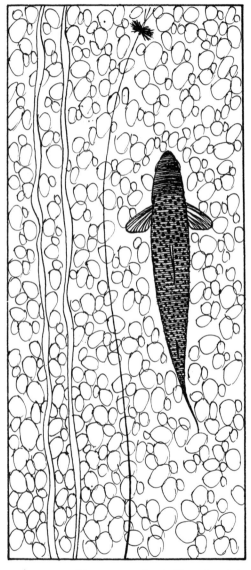

A correctly-presented fly should alight, gently, just ahead of the rising trout. If the fly lands too far ahead of the trout, the line may fall into the trout's field of vision.

Dry fly presentation

When you have to fish across the stream to the trout, you should have no problem as long as the flow is even from bank to bank.

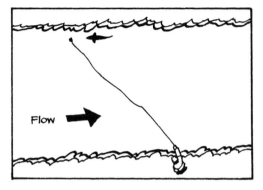

Flow

Unfortunately, conditions do not always present a perfect situation.

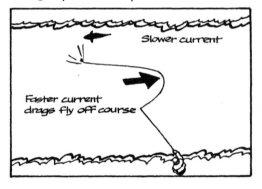

Slower current

Faster current drags fly off course

The remedy for this is to create some slack line.

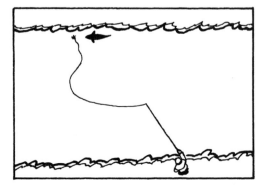

Dry fly presentation

When two or more trout are rising in close proximity to one another, care must be taken to select the fish in the correct order, to avoid scaring the other fish.

There are occasions when rises are few and far between, but this does not mean efforts with the dry fly will prove fruitless. Cover every likely-looking spot with a cast or two, and be prepared for a take just as if you had cast to a rising fish. Here are some places worth trying.

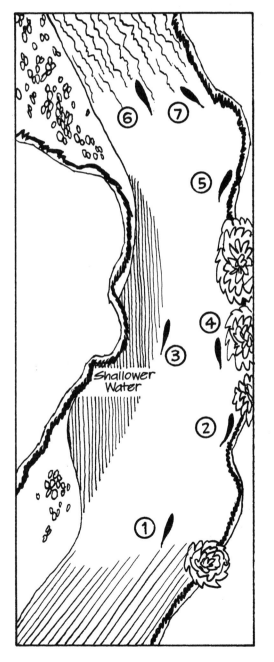

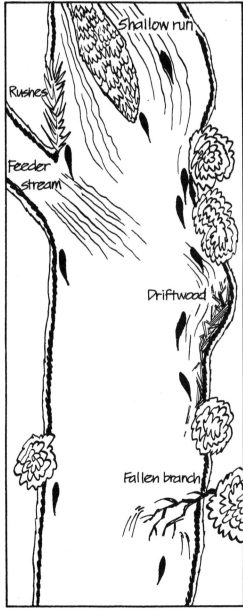

Upstream wet fly

Smaller, fast-flowing, overgrown streams are ideally suited to the upstream wet fly method.

Trout lies in a small rocky river

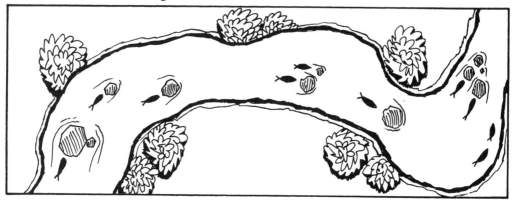

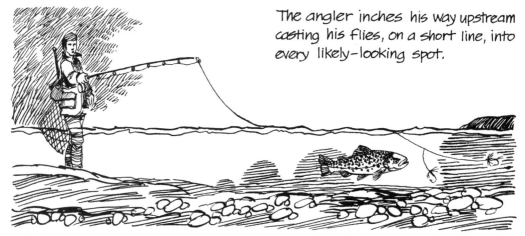

The angler inches his way upstream casting his flies, on a short line, into every likely-looking spot.

The downstream method

This method is practised with a team of, usually, three flies, similar to that used in the traditional loch method, but using smaller patterns. It is best employed on the larger, swiftly-flowing rocky rivers.

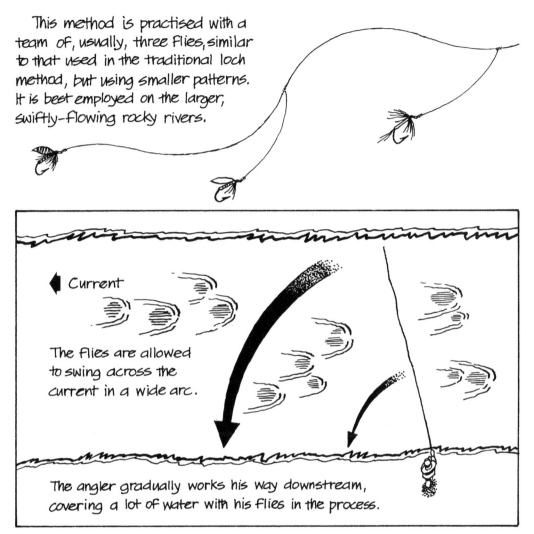

Current

The flies are allowed to swing across the current in a wide arc.

The angler gradually works his way downstream, covering a lot of water with his flies in the process.

Pay special attention to the quieter water on the downstream side of large stones.

The more sedate flow of the lowland river is ideally suited to fishing a nymph. Nymph fishing comes into its own when the trout are not feeding on the imago, but are intercepting the nymph as it swims to the surface or is being carried along in the flow of the current. If trout are 'bulging' just beneath the surface, or are showing their tails, then this is the time to tie on a nymph.

Presenting a nymph in running water

The artificial nymph is fished singly and cast upstream; in fact, the whole procedure is like dry fly fishing, except that here the nymph is meant to sink as soon as it hits the water. In nymph fishing, the avoidance of drag is not important. Nymphs are free-swimming and the trout take them as they swim in all directions.

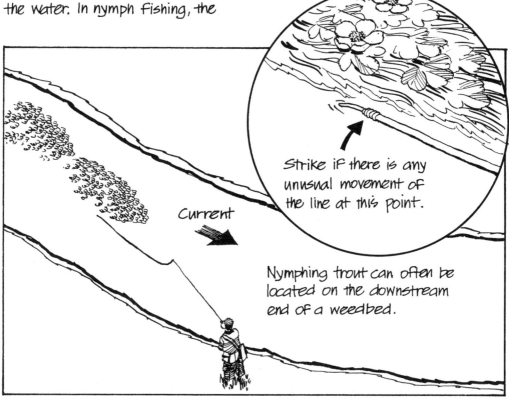

Current

Strike if there is any unusual movement of the line at this point.

Nymphing trout can often be located on the downstream end of a weedbed.

Small stream dapping

On many small streams bank-side foliage is so dense as to make ortho-dox fly presentation impossible. How-ever, the angler who uses a little init-iative and stealth, can extract trout that would make the locals gasp with astonishment.

The angler should walk slowly and quietly along the bank, or sit in a position which affords a reasonable view of the water. Eventually a trout will show itself by rising.

The angler should then take up a position directly over the fish. Conceal-ment and stealth are now even more important. The rod is poked through the foliage and the fly lowered until it touches the surface of the water. Some movement can be imparted to the fly by jiggling the rod-tip.

When the trout takes the fly, the rod-tip should be lowered before lifting into the fish.

A long-handled net is almost always necessary to extract trout from these confined places.

Ideal patterns for stream dapping.

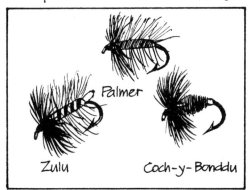

Palmer

Zulu

Coch-y-Bonddu

Stiff-actioned fly rod.

Very light fly line, No 4 is about right.

Very short leader about 6 lb (2.70 kg)

Drilled bullet, held by split shot, to pull line through rings.

Hooking

A trout taking a wet fly fished downstream in fast water will often hook itself. The angler feels the tug and the fish is on.

The take of a trout that has just accepted an upstream wet fly or a nymph is far more subtle. The best way to detect these invisible takes is to watch the point where the line joins the leader. When a take occurs the line will stop, or be drawn upstream. Then is the time to tighten on the fish.

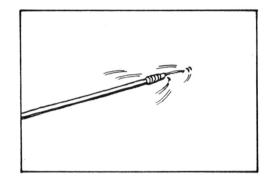

A small trout snatching at a dry fly in a fast stream needs to be struck very quickly, by flicking back the wrist.

Larger trout in slower, quieter water should be allowed to turn well down with the fly; in fact, it is often advisable to wait until the line starts to move forward. This is particularly important on the majority of still-waters.

Playing and landing

Once the hook is set, the rod-tip should be held well up. A small trout dashing around a pool in a moorland stream should prove no problem; the elasticity of the rod-tip will absorb its activity until it is ready for the net. Larger trout, however, will have to be given some line, but with a steady strain applied.

The rod-tip should be held well up.

Some anglers play a trout from the reel, while others prefer to control the fish via the line.

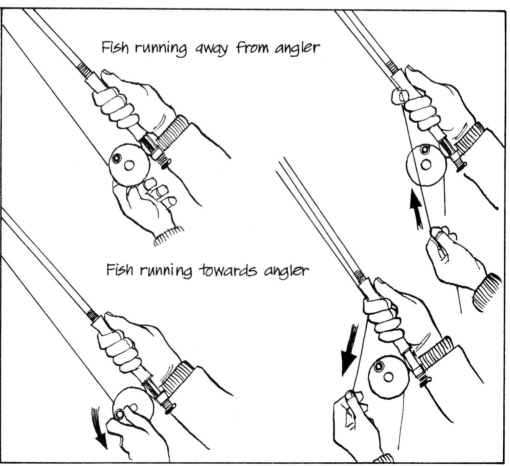

Fish running away from angler

Fish running towards angler

A fish heading for snags can be turned by applying side strain.

Playing and landing

Never attempt to net a trout before it has tired sufficiently to be controlled under the rod-tip. Adopt as low a profile as possible and avoid all unnecessary movement. Draw the fish over the stationary net. Never jab at the fish in an attempt to scoop it out.

For heavy trout, lift the net from the water using the following procedure.

Etiquette

When fishing on the bank of a lake, always position yourself at a respectable distance from the next occupied bank space.

When approaching an angler who is in the process of casting, give him a wide berth, or wait until he has completed the cast before you pass him by.

When boat fishing keep well away from other boats.

If another angler is fishing your favourite pool on the river, wait until he moves on, or walk a good distance either up or down stream before you commence fishing.

Accessories

LANDING NET : For river and small stream fishing where the angler is constantly on the move, and often up to his knees in water, a collapsible short-handled net is convenient. When fishing a lake the long-handled version is more practical.

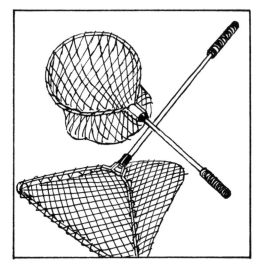

WAISTCOAT : This is a valuable piece of clothing which enables small, but important bits of equipment to be carried close to hand.

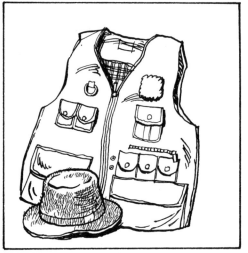

HAT: It is always advisable to wear a hat, especially when fishing a lake where long casts are often necessary ; it provides protection as well as shading the eyes.

BINOCULARS: A scan of the water surface with binoculars will often reveal the presence of feeding fish. They are also very useful for insect spotting.

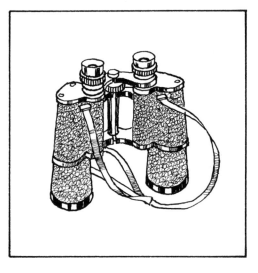

Accessories

SCISSORS: A good quality, sharp pair of scissors are essential for trimming knot ends or clipping unwanted hackle from flies. For safety's sake, stick the points into a cork.

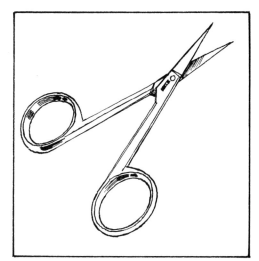

BASS BAG: These bags are sold at many stillwater fisheries, and are the ideal container for retaining your catch and keeping it fresh.

FLY WALLET

FLY BOX

STILLWATER FLY BOX

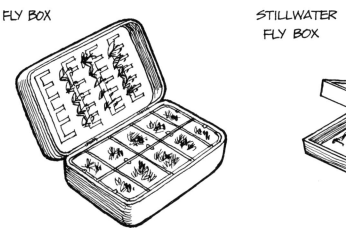

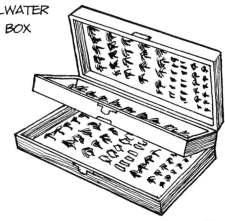

Accessories

LINE TRAY: The ideal receptacle for storing loose line during the retrieve. The alternative is to let the line fall to the ground, where it may become snagged in bank-side undergrowth. Most anglers, however, prefer to fish without a line tray.

PRIEST: The most humane way of dispatching a trout is to deal it one or two blows on the head with this impliment. Some priests are equipped with a marrow scoop. By inserting the scoop through the mouth and into the stomach of the dead trout a sample of the stomach contents can be withdrawn. A survey will quickly reveal on what insects the trout has been feeding.

Stag Horn Priest

Marrow Scoop / Priest

POLAROID GLASSES: These are invaluable for cutting out glare from the water surface. For stalking clear-water trout they are perfect, as they enable the angler to see into the water.

Knots

BLOOD KNOT: For joining lengths of different breaking strain nylon in order to produce a tapered leader. Recommended breaking strains are shown in another section of this book.

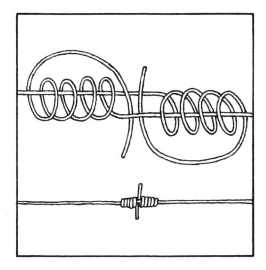

TUCKED HALF-BLOOD KNOT: Unlike the basic half-blood knot, this knot will not slip, and is the ideal knot for connecting a fly to the point or dropper of a leader.

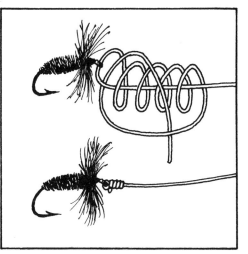

DROPPER KNOT: There is more than one knot can be used for this purpose. The water knot shown, however, permits the use of nylon equal in breaking strain to that of the point to be connected further up, where the main leader is thicker.

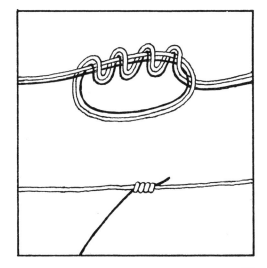

Knots

Here are three more knots which can be used to secure a fly to a leader. These knots are more suited to small dry flies — use the tucked half blood knot for larger hooks.

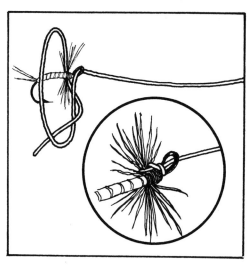

HALF HITCH

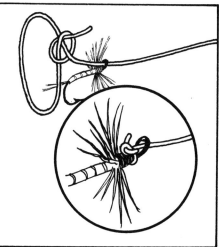

TURLE KNOT

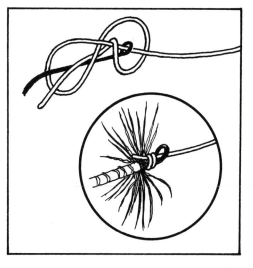

WOOD KNOT

How to cure a loose ferrule

Spigot ferrules, especially those on carbon fibre rods, tend to wear loose very quickly.

Spigot ferrule

A loose ferrule can be noticed immediately, because the male and female sections are touching one another when the rod is assembled.

To produce a tighter fit, rub the male section with candle wax.

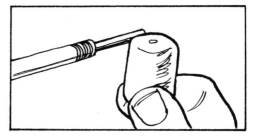

If the ferrule is very badly worn, more drastic measures will have to be taken.

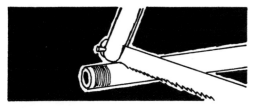

Cut about ¼ in (6 mm) from the female section, then re-whip to provide support.

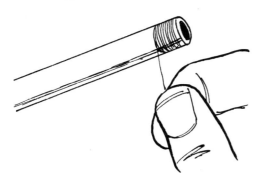

A correctly fitting spigot ferrule should look like this.

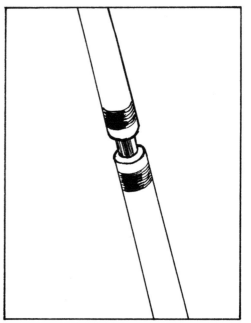

Whipping on a ring

Rods can be purchased in a half completed state, with just the handle and reel fitting secured to the blank. The rings are left to the angler. Ring positioning information is provided with the rod.

Start by securing one side of each ring to the rod. Sellotape is the ideal material for this.

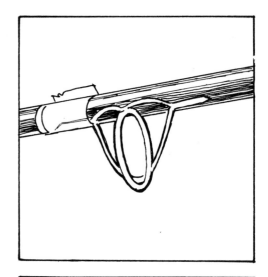

If single leg fuji rings are being used, a drop of super-glue will keep them in position, ready for whipping. Now is the time to make sure that all the rings are exactly in line.

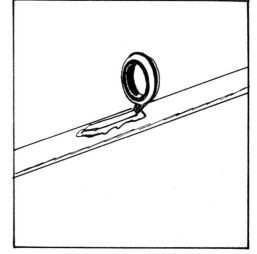

Starting at a point on the rod, just clear of the foot of the ring, wind the whipping thread back on itself for five or six turns, and cut off the tag end.

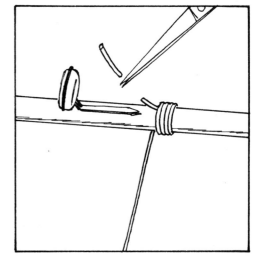

Whipping on a ring

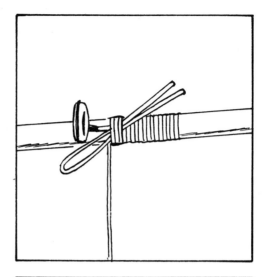

Continue whipping, making sure that the turns are tight to one another. About five turns short of where you intend to finish, insert a loop of whipping thread or nylon monofilament, and continue whipping over this loop.

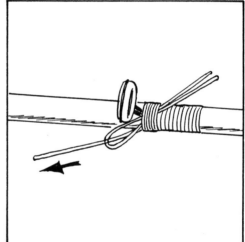

Making sure that a steady tension is being maintained, push the end of the whipping through the eye of the loop.

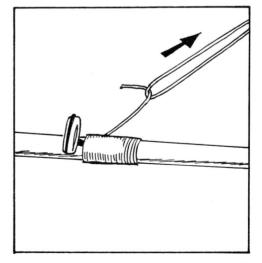

Pull the loop through the whipping, and keep pulling until the end of the whipping is completely through. Cut off the tag end.

If the ring has two feet, repeat the whole operation, after removing the sellotape. When all the rings are secured coat the whippings with two or three layers of varnish.

Licence

How to identify a salmon parr.

It is most important that, before you
go rushing off to the nearest river to
catch a trout, you are in possession
of a trout rod licence. Permission is
also needed from the riparian owner
of the land through which the river
flows. If an angling club controls the
fishing rights, a permit issued by that
club will be required.

Many private and water authority
stillwater fisheries issue block
permits which include, in the fee, the
charge for a rod licence.

A trout licence entitles the licen-
see to fish for coarse fish and trout,
but not salmon or sea trout. Salmon
parr accidently caught while trout
fishing should be returned to the
water.

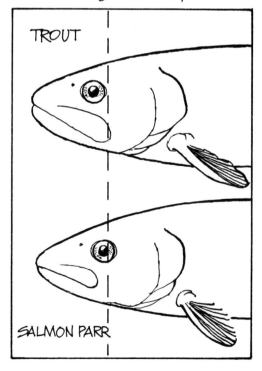

TROUT

SALMON PARR

78

Water authorities

Ten water authority areas exist in England and Wales, with each area issuing its own licence.

The itinerant angler should therefore ensure that the relevant licence is acquired, before any fishing is done.

NORTH-UMBRIAN

NORTH WEST

YORKSHIRE

SEVERN TRENT

ANGLIAN

WELSH

THAMES

WESSEX

SOUTHERN

SOUTH WEST